the japanese house

RIGHT *Entrance to Yoshida-sanso.*

Published by Tuttle Publishing, an imprint of
Periplus Editions (HK) Ltd., with editorial offices
at 364 Innovation Drive, North Clarendon,
Vermont 05759 USA

Created by Co & Bear Productions (UK) Ltd.
Copyright © 2000 Co & Bear Productions (UK) Ltd.
Photographs copyright © Noboru Murata,
represented by Uniphoto Press.

LCC Card No. 63020587
ISBN-10: 0-8048-3262-5
ISBN-13: 978-0-8048-3262-5
ISBN-13: 978-4-8053-0988-7 (for sale in Japan only)

Distributed by:

North America, Latin America & Europe
Tuttle Publishing
364 Innovation Drive
North Clarendon, VT 05759-9436 U.S.A.
Tel: 1 (802) 773-8930; Fax: 1 (802) 773-6993
info@tuttlepublishing.com
www.tuttlepublishing.com

Japan
Tuttle Publishing
Yaekari Building, 3rd Floor
5-4-12 Osaki, Shinagawa-ku
Tokyo 141 0032
Tel: (81) 03 5437-0171; Fax: (81) 03 5437-0755
tuttle-sales@gol.com

Asia Pacific
Berkeley Books Pte. Ltd.
61 Tai Seng Avenue, #02-12
Singapore 534167
Tel: (65) 628011330; Fax: (65) 628016290
inquiries@periplus.com.sg
www.periplus.com

10 09 08
12 11 10 9 8

Printed in Singapore

the japanese house

architecture and interiors

photography by noboru murata

written by alexandra black

TUTTLE PUBLISHING
Tokyo • Rutland, Vermont • Singapore

contents

the japanese aesthetic

The ancient Taoist scholar Laotse espoused that the true beauty of a room lay in the vacant space enclosed by the roof and walls, rather than the roof and walls themselves. He aspired to an aesthetic ideal of emptiness. True beauty could only be realised in the material world, he held, when it was stripped almost bare, with only the merest suggestion of colour, pattern or texture. The mind, the imagination of the beholder, should be allowed to complete the picture in the mood of the moment.

This is the essence of the Japanese house. Laotse's philosophy was imported to Japan via Zen Buddhism, and went on to become an integral aspect of the Japanese approach to living. The Japanese house thus shuns the decorative, the obvious, the extravagantly showy, in favour of restraint, of emptiness, or what contemporary architects and designers would refer to as minimalism.

When entering a Japanese house for the first time, it is emptiness that first strikes the foreign eye. No art works on the wall, no thick carpets, no bold wallpapers or chandeliers or heavy curtains. The house appears to have been pared back to its essential elements. It seems to be purely functional.

The second thing that becomes apparent is its impermanent state. Interior walls slide open to double the size of a room. At night, futons are pulled from sliding cupboards, built flush with the wall, and put away again in the morning to clear floor space for other uses. From season to season, this mutability becomes even more obvious. In summer, external walls are slid open to bring a sense of the garden beyond inside, as well as

cooling breezes. Sliding wooden *shoji* are replaced with ones of bamboo or reed in summer, to improve ventilation. And from summer to autumn to winter to spring, small decorative details mark the passing of the seasons: the scroll in the living-room alcove is changed, or a new flower arrangement appears in the entrance, bearing a blossom or sprig evocative of the time of year. There are many ways of describing the Japanese house in detail; of approaching its different architectural and interior components. The garden, the veranda, the sliding walls, or the tatami floor: any one could be discussed from any number of viewpoints. They could be explained historically – how each element evolved as the result of religious beliefs, of political events, or artistic trends. Or they might be analysed for their adaptation to a hot, humid summer climate and earthquake-prone geography.

Yet again, they could be explained practically in terms of the builders' craft, or mathematically in terms of their scale and proportion. However, any real understanding of the Japanese house must begin with an appreciation of the materials used in its building. Just as brick and plaster gave European towns their particular appearance, so have wood, bamboo, straw and paper lent Japanese towns and villages their unique look and a powerful sense of continuity that is still evident today, despite the dramatic changes to the landscape and urban fabric of the past half-century.

architectural elements

tatami

More than any other component of the Japanese house, tatami is the core around which almost all residential architecture revolves. In essence a floor covering woven from straw, the rectangular tatami mat is found in almost every house in the country. Even modern homes will include one tatami room; essentially a tea room, but also a guest room where futons can be unfurled at night.

The origin of tatami stretches back to ancient Japanese civilisation, when straw was spread over a bare earth floor to provide softness and warmth. In the Heian period (794–1185), this device evolved into movable throw mats, which could be laid down anywhere in the house as needed, to sleep on or to sit on around the hearth. In the fifteenth century, tatami became a permanent covering for the entire floor of a room. The dimensions of the tatami mat were determined to accommodate a person lying down. Although the measurements have fluctuated over the centuries, today a typical tatami is about 90 centimetres wide and 180 centimetres long.

As a flooring material, tatami is eminently suited to its climate. It allows air to circulate around the floor, it is soft and welcoming underfoot. Needless to say, the custom of removing one's shoes inside is in good part intended to help keep the tatami in pristine condition.

Tatami, though, is more than a flooring device, in fact it regulates the size of the Japanese house and the dimensions within it. Street frontages, room sizes, spaces between pillars and other interior structures were, and still are, measured in terms of tatami mats. This style of

modular living is uniquely Japanese and has been hugely influential on architects around the world.

bamboo

Historical texts reveal that in Japan bamboo once had over 1400 practical and decorative uses. In the Japanese house, bamboo is a common and expected feature. A bamboo fence is often the first point of contact between the street and the rest of the house. Bamboo is also the favoured material for the ceilings and rafters of traditional farmhouses and country dwellings.

Bamboo, or sometimes reed, is used to fashion the external blinds, called *sudare,* that shield the façade of a house from the intense heat of the sun, and which replace *shoji* doors in summer to aid ventilation. Bamboo's

strength and durability, its suppleness, its ability to split straight, and also be woven, have made it much prized by carpenters and builders.

Aside from its great advantages as a construction and craft material, bamboo also carries great aesthetic value. It exudes a raw, natural beauty in its knotted joints and its smooth glossy rounded surface. It also evokes the gentle beauties of nature – the sound of a bamboo forest clacking and rustling in the breeze is one of the most evocative in the collective sensory experience of Japan, recurring in literature, poetry and film.

Consequently the use of bamboo as a decorative device, as opposed to a construction material, is widespread. In the tea room, one of the pillars is often bamboo; the water dipper and the tea whisks are also of bamboo, lending both

lightness and a sense of rusticity. The flower arrangement in an alcove or in the entrance to a house may be in a basket of bamboo.

paper

Novelist Junichiro Tanizaki wrote that 'the beauty of a Japanese room depends on a variation of shadows, heavy shadows against light shadows. Westerners are amazed at the simplicity of Japanese rooms, perceiving in them no more than ashen walls bereft of ornament. Their reaction is understandable, but it betrays a failure to comprehend the mystery of shadows.'

This mystery of shadows is in fact engineered by the expert use of paper as a building and decorative material. It is handmade paper, or *washi,* that gives the Japanese

house its moody and atmospheric interior. There are hundreds of handmade papers each suited to a particular purpose depending on its character. In the house, there are three particular applications for paper worth noting. Interior windows and sliding *shoji* doors are fitted with a heavy opaque paper in creamy-white, softening the light as it enters a room from outside. Smoother coloured and patterned papers are used to cover *fusuma,* the solid doors that divide rooms and conceal cupboard space. And more delicate *washi* covers the traditional floor lamps called *andon,* which cast a delicate glow around the house at night.

wood

Perhaps the most precious and revered of all materials, wood has until the late twentieth century been the most

accessible of materials, cut from the forests that cover Japan's mountainous interior. Pine, cedar and cypress trees have all grown in abundance, although these woods are now increasingly viewed as a finite, restricted and expensive resource.

Nevertheless, most house construction is still based on a timber framework as it has been for centuries, and the carpenter is the most respected of artisans. While massive ancient temples and shrines, built entirely from wood, have withstood a millennium, most residential architecture has always been of a much lighter, more temporary nature – perhaps a necessary precaution in an earthquake-prone land.

Wood, however, is much more than simply a building material. In interiors, its warmth, its irregularities and texture are considered important aesthetic elements.

stone

The heaviest of the materials involved in creating a Japanese house, stone is reserved very much for the exterior parts of the building. It is used invisibly for the foundations, and very visibly for pathways, entranceways and gardens.

Stone, like timber, is valued for its individuality. Single large rocks can form the centrepiece of a Japanese garden – the peculiar colouring, texture and shape of each one contributing significantly to the mood of the landscaping. Flat, irregular-shaped pieces of stone are used for footpaths and to pave entranceways. When scrubbed or hosed with water – shining in the early morning sun, or glowing in the light of a lantern – stone can take on poetic qualities.

茶室

Tea, it has been said, lies at the root of Japanese culture – the rituals and philosophy associated with tea-drinking having spread to influence aesthetics profoundly over the course of a thousand years. From calligraphy to ceramics, from flower arranging to gardens to architecture, very little has escaped its impact. As the arena in which the tea ceremony takes place, the teahouse symbolises the very ideals of tea philosophy.

Introduced to Japan around the tenth century by Zen priests returning from studies in China, tea was used primarily by Buddhist monks to help keep them awake during long hours of meditation, but its serving had already devleoped in China into a ritual of deep spiritual significance. In Japan, however, the spiritual dimension of tea extended beyond the religious order to the secular world – in effect creating a cult of aestheticism.

The intricacies of the tea ceremony and the aesthetics associated with it reached their apotheosis in the sixteenth century under the tea master Sen Rikyu Soeki. He is credited with formalising the tea ceremony, and setting in place a strict framework for every element linked to it, from the type of teacups used to the flowers displayed, to the structure and materials of the teahouse. In establishing the first teahouse, Soeki set out to create a space that would emphasise the fragile and temporary nature of life. It was intended to recreate the world of the spirit by evoking the simplicity and artlessness of a straw hut, albeit in a highly stylised way.

Decoration was kept minimal, the better to focus the minds of those particpating in the tea ceremony. Only a few key objects were permitted – a scroll, some flowers, and the tea kettle and cups themselves. The

overriding aesthetic concern was to create a sense of *wabi* – a refined rusticity that is seen as uniquely Japanese. *Wabi* has been the preoccupation of every tea master, teahouse builder and craftsman since the sixteenth century.

Little has changed since the teahouses of Sen Rikyu's time. Indeed the major tea schools in Japan are founded on his teachings, and their teahouses are built according to his tenets. One of the leading Kyoto schools is Mushakoji Senke, founded by one of Rikyu's ancestors in the seventeenth century. The school's complex of tea rooms and gardens is one of the best places to appreciate the beauty of teahouse architecture, and to understand the principles of *wabi* that underpin Japan's decorative arts.

On entering the Kansuien, the teahouse most often used at Mushakoji Senke, the guest is first struck by both the simplicity of the materials used in its construction, and the fact that nothing seems symmetrical. This irregularity is very much part of the *wabi* aesthetic – a device that is purposefully used to suggest an apparent carelessness; as though the house has evolved organically, rather than in a carefully considered fashion. The rough, raw materials are also specfically chosen to give the same impression. The low ceilings of thatched rice straw, the bamboo pillars, the untreated, unadorned clay walls, the tatami mat floors, the paper-covered windows – all work to convey a feeling of lightness, fragility and evanescence. Together they create the ideal environment, where interest and tension are held through the contrast between the simple, natural elements used in the construction and the highly ritualised and formalised play of the tea ceremony itself.

⊞ LEFT & ABOVE *The garden is a crucial element of the tea house, as is clear at the Mushakoji Senke tea school. A simple stone path leads from an outdoor waiting pavilion to a number of different tearooms, each used for different purposes and at different times of the year. The* roji, *or garden path, symbolises the transition from the mundane world to the spiritually enlightened world of the tea ceremony. While appearing artless, the teahouse garden is beautifully maintained – piles of pine needles are raked into 'ponds' of red and gold, and the stepping stones are doused with water to give them a glistening sheen.*

ABOVE *A paved stone path leads the visitor from the informal*
entrance gate to the main part of the tea school. More than just
a directional pointer, the path is an important element in the
design of any teahouse, and in the process of the tea ceremony
itself. According to one tea master of the fifteenth century:
'From the moment you enter the garden pathway until the time
you depart, you should hold the host in most respectful esteem,
in the spirit that the gathering will occur but once in your life.'

OPPOSITE *A stone wrapped in black cord traditionally acts as*
a stop sign, signalling that access is prohibited. Here in the tea-
house garden, though, it is used more for its ornamental effect.

OPPOSITE & LEFT *Purity and cleanliness are crucial components of any tea ceremony, and all the utensils must be carefully cleaned and prepared before use. This takes place in the* midsuya, *or anteroom, which is screened from the view of the guest. Typical utensils required for the ceremony include an iron tea kettle, a tea caddy, tea scoop, containers for fresh water and waste water, flower vase, teacups, whisks and plates on which to serve the traditional accompanying sweet, called* o-kashi.

OPPOSITE & ABOVE *This garden gate is one of the symbols of the Mushakoji Senke tea school, and marks the entrance to the Kankyuan tea room. The gate is called Amigasamon because the roof resembles an* amigasa, *a large rain hat made of woven bamboo (*Mon *means 'gate' in Japanese.)*

ABOVE *One of the smallest tea rooms at Mushakoji Senke, and the most informal, the Gyoshutei (Gliding Boat Hall) is so called because the ceiling resembles the hull of a boat. The ceiling and the raised window overlooking the garden are meant to evoke a summer boat trip on the river.*

 FAR LEFT & NEAR LEFT *The shoji screens of this tea room slide back to reveal the garden, providing a meditative view for the guests of the tea ceremony. The entire scene captures the sense of calm simplicity which is crucial to the tea ceremony, offering an escape from the troubled outside world.*

NEAR LEFT, BELOW *The window in teahouse architecture serves not only to control the strength of light admitted inside, but also as a decorative and artistic device. Here a* shoji *window is topped with an arch inset with rustic-style latticework – it is one of several elaborate window forms found in the teahouse.*

BELOW & RIGHT *The Kansuien tea room contains the essential elements of tea ceremony aesthetics: the* tokonoma *alcove, with its rough-hewn wooden pillar, calligraphed scroll and discreet flower; the recessed hearth, where a brazier smoulders; and a wooden container of charcoal, with a single white feather to dust away fallen ash.*

街の家

the townhouse

When the aesthetics and construction of the teahouse were perfected by the great tea master Sen Rikyu Soeki in the Muromachi era (1333–1573), few could have imagined just how far-reaching its influence would be. To begin with, the newly popular practice of tea ceremony generated an explosion in the arts and crafts, particularly in Kyoto, which was at the time the Imperial capital. Potters were busy making tea bowls, or *chawan*, ironworkers forging kettles, basket weavers fashioning bamboo tea whisks, and lacquerware makers turning out exquisite tea caddies and tableware. Those in the business of construction were also much in demand: carpenters, tatami-makers and gardeners worked non-stop to cater to the new teahouse trend.

Eventually, the style of the teahouse found its way into mainstream architecture. It was first adopted by the samurai class, who felt that its spiritual dimensions were ideally suited to their own noble and altruistic goals. The samurais evolved an architectural blueprint known as *shoin,* and this in turn spawned another style known as *sukiya* – which again owed much to the teahouse. Where the *shoin* style could only be used strictly by the samurai class, *sukiya*-style houses could be built by anyone with money to afford the cost of the skilled carpenters and other artisans required.

The Kyoto townhouse of Nakamura Sotetsu is a fine example of the way in which the elegant *sukiya* style has infused residential architecture. Appropriately, Sotetsu herself is a renowned lacquerware maker, whose pieces are found in the most prestigious teahouses, as well as in private and museum collections. As with most

街
の
家

Japanese artists and artisans, Sotetsu's craft has been handed down through her family for generations. The family has lived on the same site for over 400 years, although the present house was built by her great-grandfather and renovated by Sotetsu in recent years. In the early part of the Edo period (1603–1867), when the royal court of Kyoto was at its height, Sotetsu's ancestors were commissioned to create elegant lacquer pieces for weddings, banquets and the tea ceremonies that were an almost daily event at the palace. Sotetsu now continues the tradition of making beautiful tea ceremony pieces, working from her home studio.

Interestingly, the first room on entering the house is a tea room. As is typical, there are two doorways. One, a full-height set of sliding *shoji* screens is the *kijin-guchi,* or noble's entrance, which harks back to the days of strict class segregation. The second is a half-height sliding *shoji,* known as a *nijiru-guchi* through which one must enter on hands and knees – a humbling act that prepares the mind for tea ceremony. The ceiling of the tea room is characteristic of the *sukiya* style. It is fashioned from *ajiro,* a type of woven bark, and creates a distinctly rustic air, as do the walls, which are in a roughly finished clay called *juraku.* The design forms here – the strategically understated materials and the asymmetrical layout – set the standard for the rest of the house. In each room, though, there is always some individualistic element, reflecting the personal taste of the owner. Her exquisite lacquerware is invariably present, whether in the form of a bowl or dinner setting, the edging on a hearth, the shelf in a *tokonoma* or a beautifully wrought table.

 ABOVE *The entrance to the house leads to the tea room. The approach from the front gate creates an immediate atmosphere of restraint and tranquillity and from the outset binds the house and garden into a unified whole. The tea room can be entered directly from the garden through the* nijiru-guchi, *an opening just large enough to crawl through. The device dates back to samurai times and compelled warriors to remove their swords and humble themselves before entering the tea room.*

LEFT *The tea room walls are rendered in a rough clay-like finish, while parts of the ceiling are woven from bark. The supporting post in the* tokonoma *alcove is of red pine.*

ABOVE RIGHT *The interior mood of refined rusticity begins in the garden, the entrance to which is marked by a finely crafted bamboo fence and gate.*

BELOW RIGHT & RIGHT *Looking out over the garden, the main living room is flooded with natural light, enhancing the warm tones of the tatami floor. In summer the sliding doors slide across to give direct access to the leafy garden, while in winter a set of* shoji *screens can be added to provide insulation from the cold.*

LEFT *Guests and clients are received in the main reception room. On close inspection this plain tatami room reveals a wealth of detail, such as the lacquerware table and lacquer bowls, all made by Nakamura Sotetsu. An antique Japanese doll sits in the alcove, and one from Bali lies on the veranda.*

ABOVE *A square, unadorned tray with three matching bowls for rice, soup and a meat or vegetable dish, together with a red sake cup. Although plain in appearance, such pieces are works of art, used for special occasions. They are fashioned in solid wood and finished with glossy lacquer.*

LEFT *A rare glimpse into the intimate world of an artist. In her studio upstairs, Nakamura Sotetsu crafts exquisite lacquerware pieces, ranging from perfectly simple rice bowls in plain black or red lacquer, to the most elegant and expensive inlaid utensils for tea ceremony. Sotetsu's family have been making such pieces for more than four centuries. Usually the craft is handed down to father and son, but in a family of daughters Sotetsu, as the eldest, inherited the mantle from her father.*

 ABOVE *Nakamura Sotetsu began studying lacquerware-making as a child, formally taking up her apprenticeship at nineteen. Her expertise is clearly evident in the* rikkyu, *or tea caddies, she crafts, all of which are made specially to order. One of her three daughters is now also a lacquer artist.*

OPPOSITE *The artist's studio is a small, light-filled space, which can be screened off with sliding doors for complete privacy. With its rough wooden shelving and old panelled cupboard, the space appears surprisingly humble given the priceless pieces of lacquerware, called* urushi, *created here.*

美山荘

舟 mountain refuge

There are few places that grip the Japanese psyche as the mountains do. They are not only a dominant geographical feature of the island nation – some ninety percent of the country is forested alps – they are also deeply symbolic. Mount Fuji is a national icon, and the Shinto spirits of ancient ancestors are still held to dwell in mountain peaks. As in many other cultures, the mountains are also seen as a place for escape, for embracing nature and for entering a meditative, spiritual realm.

Aesthetically, too, the mountains play an important part in visual culture – from the mountain scenes depicted on hand-painted screens to the ubiquitous autumn leaf of the maple trees that cover alpine slopes, to the mountain home itself. Mountain houses vary greatly in character. Many are built in the style of the farmhouse, with solid wooden beams and thick thatched roofs suited to a cold and snowy climate. Some mountain dwellings are little more than huts, providing shelter for pilgrims in times past, and weekend hikers in modern times. Occasionally, though, one comes across a house that is far more rarefied in both function and design.

Miyama-sou is an aesthete's retreat. It is a simple but elegant structure – clearly intended as a place from which the mountains can be admired, a place for drinking in nature – not its raw state, but in a managed way that is so characteristic of the Japanese approach to the natural world. Miyama-sou was built in the mid-nineteenth century by the current owner's great grandfather as an inn where pilgrims to the nearby Buddhist temple, Bujoji, could spend the night. Yet Miyama-sou's refinement indicates that these pilgrims were no rough

美
山
荘

peasants. They might well have come just for the experience of staying in this charming inn, an experience equally enriching to the spirit as a visit to the temple itself.

At first sight, Miyama-sou appears unpreposessing. Set in the hilly folds of Mount Daihizan, north of Kyoto, a small building perched on the banks of a stream and surrounded by a thicket of cherry trees, it would be easy to pass by without a second look. But closer inspection reveals an abode of great elegance. It boasts a refined rusticity apparently influenced by the *wabi* sensibility of the Buddhist tea ceremony. With its understated presence, its irregular and asymmetrical architectural features and its mix of the raw with the highly sophisticated, the inn is a delightful example of the tea-inspired *sukiya* style, in a most unexpected location.

The entrance is approached down a path paved with massive slabs of mountain stone, at night lit by candlelit rice-paper lamps placed at foot level. At the end of the path, the *genkan* waits invitingly – its beautiful screens and circular window indicating that this is no humble mountain shelter. The round window, or *maruma-do*, is a device characteristic of of temple and aristocratic architecture, and historically marks the transition from the window as a practical feature for letting in light to a decorative and artistic feature. And it thus gives Miyama-sou an immediate air of distinction. Inside, too, particular features stamp this inn with great individual-ity – the bathroom with its traditional *hinoki* tub overlooking the stream outside; the delicately carved transoms in the tatami rooms; and the fantastically patterned *fusuma* doors.

 **LEFT** *Miyama-sou is almost invisible under the deep drifts of winter snow that regularly blanket the mountains north of Kyoto. This low-set single-storey house may not look remarkable from the outside, but as the first-time visitor approaches it becomes clear that it is designed with a very precise aesthetic in mind.*

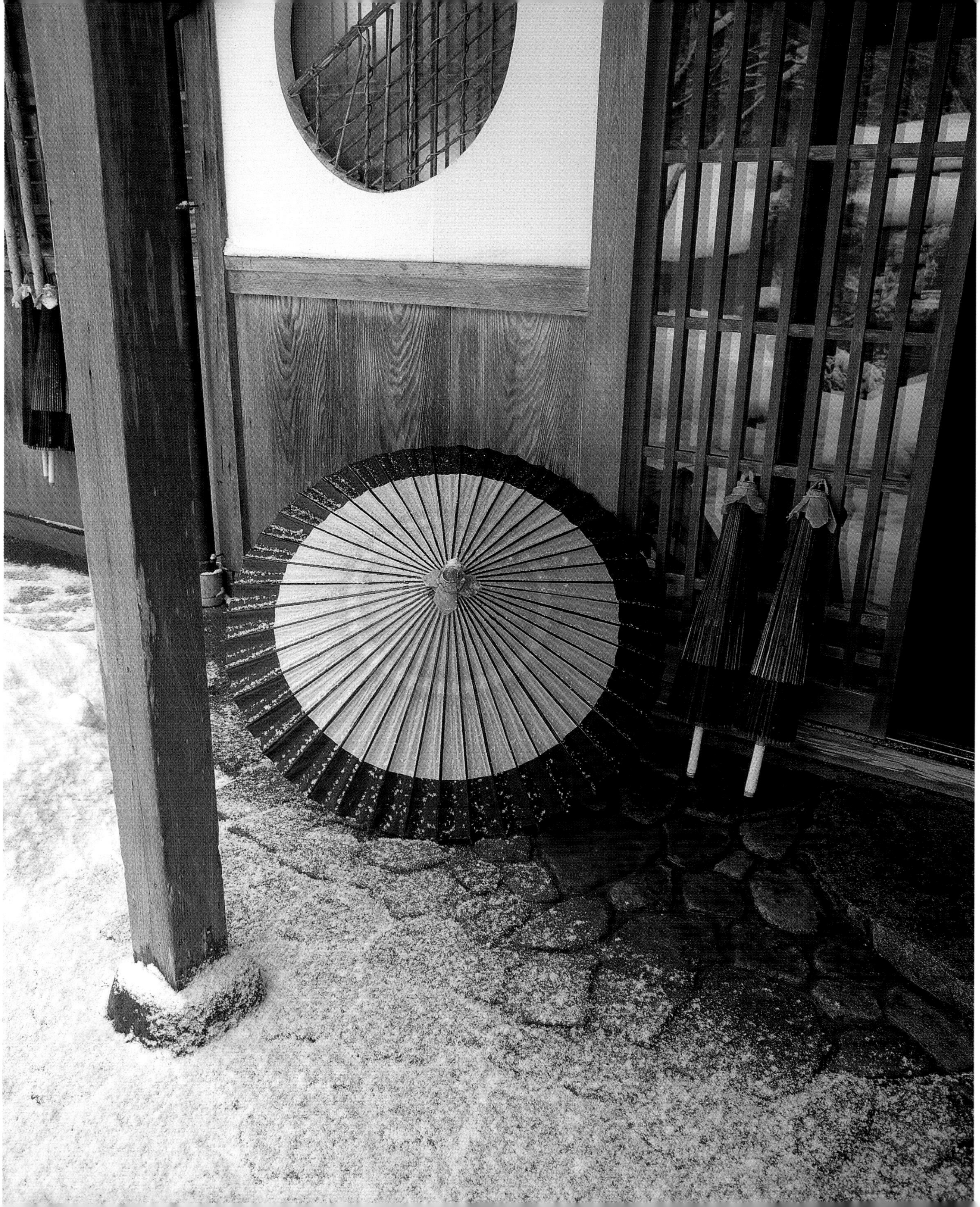

⛩ **OPPOSITE** *Handmade oiled-paper umbrellas, a speciality of Kyoto, sit ready at the entrance for those who venture out into the falling snow. These large rain umbrellas are called* bangasa *and the best-quality ones are made to last for years.*

BELOW *Even under the weight of deep winter snows, there is no mistaking the elegant entrance to Miyama-sou, with its circular window, freshly swept stone-paved path and porch, and the gentle glimmer of light from inside the* genkan, *or foyer.*

BELOW *The genkan, or foyer, presents a picture of spare and restrained elegance. Details such as the ribbing on the wooden* amado *shutters, and the subtle, beautifully coloured paper-covered doors beyond, point to an interior of great refinement.*

OPPOSITE & OVERLEAF *The most distinctive features of Miyama-sou's guest rooms are the delightful hand-painted papers that cover the sliding screens, called* fusuma, *and the decoratively carved transoms above, which gently filter the light.*

ABOVE *Atmospheric lighting is critical in creating the right ambience at Miyama-sou and, indeed, in any Japanese house. Opaque* shoji *doors and windows soften the natural light from outside, while shades fashioned from handmade paper create a soft, non-directional glow from electric lights.*

OPPOSITE *In contrast to the vibrant* fusuma *screens, with their evocations of the natural world, the rest of the decor is left intentionally bare, so as not to distract from the scenes of nature outside. Guests sit on slim cushions, called* zabuton, *and enjoy a restorative tea while admiring the view.*

RIGHT & BELOW *The architectural mix of rustic and refined elements extends to even the smallest details. Here (right) a cup of* hoji-cha *tea sits beside an antique smoking kit – in times past proffered as the traditional welcome to any guest – while a sweet rice cake is served alongside a cup of* matcha, *the powdered whisked green tea served at tea ceremonies (below).*

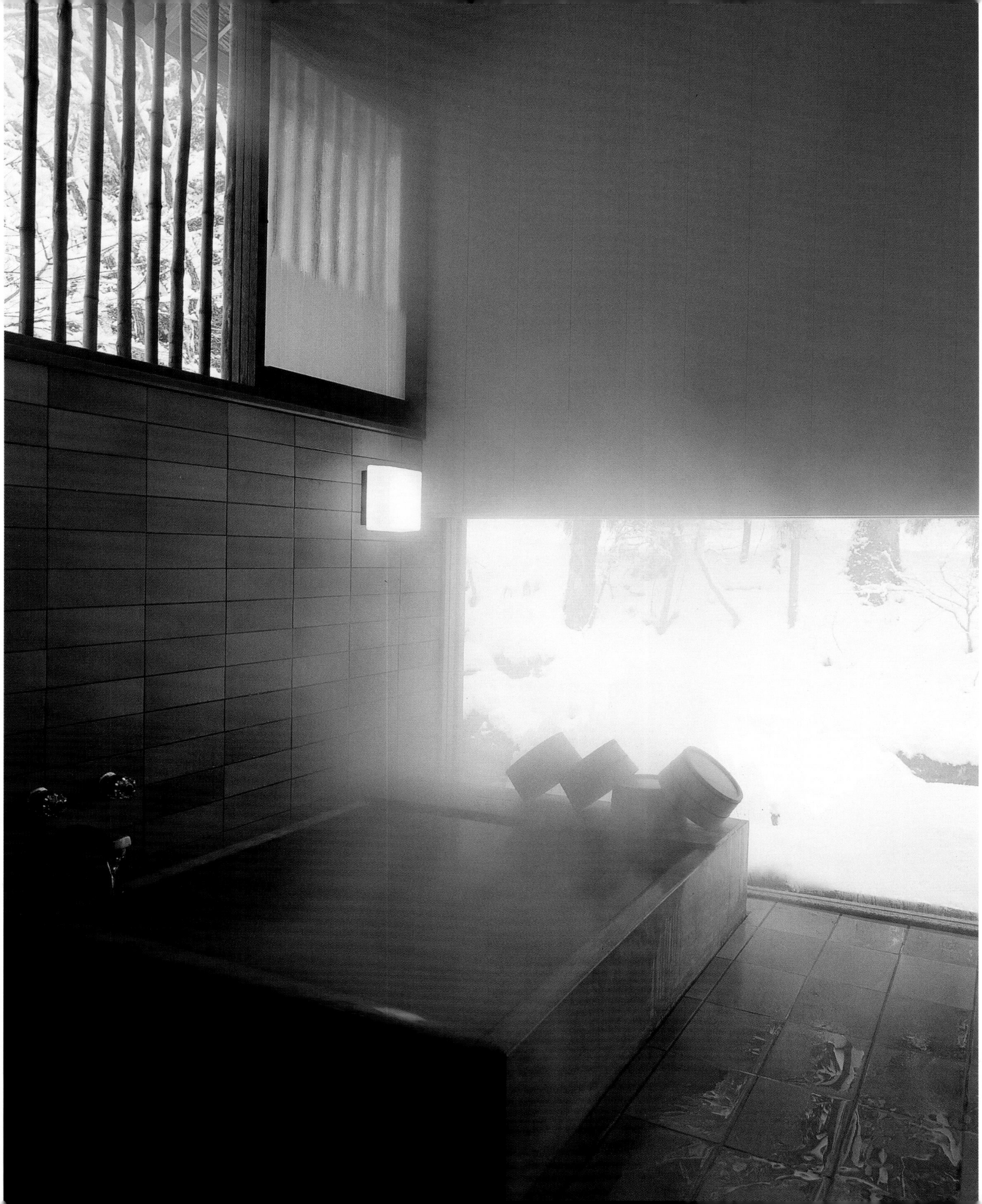

OPPOSITE *This wooden tub of Japanese cypress overlooks a snow-covered forest to create the most tranquil of environments for bathing. The cypress tub – with matching buckets and stools – produces a distinctive scent, evocative of the trees outside.*

BELOW *In winter the outer wall of the* engawa, *or veranda, would typically be formed by a series of heavy wooden shutters that slide across to meet in the middle. Here, though, they have been removed to offer guests a panoramic view of the snow.*

京都町家

kyoto machiya

One of the most significant achievements of the Edo period, which spanned more than 250 years from 1603 to 1867, was the development of the *machiya*, or city house. The emergence of this distinctive architectural form coincided with a period of great national peace and prosperity as well as Japan's self-imposed isolation from the rest of the world. The impact on the country's arts and architecture was enormous.

The key to the explosion in creative culture was the newly emergent merchant class. As they prospered throughout the Edo period, they spent their wealth as patrons of the arts, buying richly painted screens, *ukiyo-e* wood-block prints, elegant porcelain, inlaid lacquerware and exquisite silks. To try to contain the increasing power of the merchants, the ruling shogunate introduced strict laws governing the construction and decoration of the merchant *machiya*. Any extravagant displays of wealth were forbidden, and the structures themselves adhered to a uniform code.

Earlier forms of *machiya* had long existed in previous centuries. They had functioned as the building blocks of close-knit neighbourhoods, which banded together for protection against regular civil wars and attacks from feuding warlords. Taxes, levied according to the width of street frontage, encouraged the building of long, thin houses. During the Edo era, they evolved further as rich merchants sought to improve their lifestyles with elegant interior touches and pleasure gardens. Traditional *machiya* from this period are now few and far between. The best examples can be found in Kyoto, especially in the inner neighbourhoods, where pockets of

京都町家

merchants have plied their trade for centuries. Several common exterior features make the *machiya* easy to spot. They display a remarkable harmony in their façades and proportion, thanks to an age-old construction system based on the unit of a single tatami mat (around 90cm x 180cm). Typically they are two-storeyed, dark wooden structures – Edo laws prohibited merchants from building higher – with the façade at ground level and the upper level consisting of slatted windows called *koshimado*. These gave an element of privacy and seclusion from busy streets outside yet still allowed plenty of ventilation during the hot, sticky Kyoto summers.

Inside, too, the interior layout conforms to a uniform pattern. The sliding door at street level opens to a *toriniwa* – a long corridor, usually paved in stone, which runs the entire depth of the house and reaches to roof height. All the rooms in the house open from the *toriniwa*, and are raised 30 to 50 centimetres for optimum ventilation. Business was conducted in the shop room at the front of the house, while further back the *zashiki*, or reception room, could be used for entertaining clients or for more formal family occasions.

The *zashiki* usually overlooks an interior garden, where the owner could carve out his own piece of paradise, a place to escape the pressure of business and the heat of the summer. Beyond is one of the *machiya's* most important assets – the *kura*, or storehouse. Often there was more than one, depending on an individual's wealth. With its massive walls, thick wooden doors and tiny decorative windows, the storehouse could be used to keep food, family valuables, or the merchant's all-important stock in trade.

LEFT & ABOVE *This typical Kyoto
machiya was built in 1899 and has been
lovingly restored by the president of the
Kyoto Machiya Preservation Committee.
Despite a narrow façade at street level,
the house runs back to occupy a substantial
site, with beautifully landscaped garden and
three whitewashed kura, or storehouses.*

ABOVE *The* kura, *or storehouse, of the* machiya *is built with cedar cladding at ground level and white mortar covering the upper level. Deep-set windows, called* takamado, *are just big enough to provide ventilation. Their design is unique to the* kura.

OPPOSITE *Storehouses were built as separate structures to protect valuables from fire, in particular. This* machiya *boasts three storehouses: one for foodstuffs, one for furnishings and art, and one to safeguard the merchant's kimono silks.*

OPPOSITE & LEFT
*Once inside the front door,
the merchant's shop can be
entered directly, while a path
leads to the main part of the
house. A water well with
overhead pulley was typically
located here.*

BELOW LEFT *Beyond the*
noren *curtain marking the
entrance to the house, a path
opens out into the* toriniwa,
*or corridor, with its full-height
ceilings. All the interior rooms
open off this central corridor.*

BELOW *The zashiki, or reception room, overlooks a landscaped garden – a place for viewing rather than working or sitting in. Sudare, or reed blinds, hang the length of the engawa, or veranda, and can be unfurled in summer to give shade from the sun.*

OPPOSITE *One wall of the zashiki is occupied by a niche containing shelves and an adjoining tokonoma alcove. This device began in the tea room as a space for displaying objects for aesthetic appreciation, but soon became widespread in residential architecture.*

 LEFT & RIGHT *The zashiki, or reception room, of the traditional merchant's house takes on the quality of a stage set, in which decorative elements are changed according to the scene that will be played out in the room – whether a seasonal, formal or informal, business or private occasion. Hanging in the* tokonoma, *the scroll – with its delicately inked sprigs of pink cherry blossom – is evocative of spring. Beneath the scroll is a small but perfectly formed incense burner.*

田舎家

⊞ t h e   c o u n t r y   h o u s e

Farmers hold an almost mythic position in Japanese society. Seen as the custodians of the nation's all-important rural traditions and the backbone of its food supply, they are as romanticised as the American cowboy, or the English sheep farmer. In touch with the seasons, and the spirit world governing fertility and fortune, the Japanese farmer is caretaker of the nation's spiritual values. By association, the farmhouse is perceived as a most romantic dwelling. The steep thatched roof, the deep eaves, the long veranda with its views of the rice fields, the exposed beams and pillars inside, and the open hearth for cooking – all evoke a particular sense of nostalgia.

In reality, of course, farm life is far from romantic. In the traditional Japanese farmhouse, the winters can be bitterly cold and the summers unbearably hot. As farmers have prospered, they have understandably wasted little time in modernising their homes, installing them with the latest comforts and appliances. Farmhouse heritage and rustic aesthetics are not areas of great concern. Occasionally, clusters of old farmhouses have been bought up by local governments and kept for posterity's sake. Even more unusual is the restoration of an old farmhouse in private hands. Kiyo and Douglas Woodruff have done just that – sacrificing convenience for a taste of rural Japanese life as it once might have been.

While not farmers themselves, the Woodruffs have a keen affinity with the architecture and interior mood of the *minka*, or farmhouse. When they came across a farmhouse in a broad valley of rice fields in the Tamba region of central Japan, it was in desperate need of attention. The interior timbers were covered in soot,

and a number of unsympathetic additions – such as aluminium sliding doors in place of the original wooden ones – needed to be undone. For Douglas, an experienced carpenter who works on restoration projects as well as crafting his own furniture, the restoration of the farmhouse was an appealing, if daunting, prospect. Over the past twenty years he and his wife have gradually returned the house to something like its original state. Only the thatched roof is missing, now replaced with tin by an over-eager landlord. Yet even the absence of this feature has not detracted from the rustic ambience the house exudes. The layout is typical of a Tamba farmhouse, the tatami rooms opening off the central living space to form an L-shape around the perimeter of the house.

The play of light and shadow – an integral element of the Japanese interior – is key to the atmosphere created inside. The movable screens which open from the central living space to the exterior rooms and the veranda beyond, allow daylight to filter through and be adjusted to any strength. In the evening, electric light is banished in favour of candlelit *andon*, or floor lamps.

Under this subtle and moody lighting, the natural timbers of the farmhouse interior truly shine. Some of them are original – cypress pillars and pine beams, for example. Other wood surfaces, such as on a rich red cherry table or a low cedar table, are equally aged. They have been reclaimed and recycled by Douglas into furnishings of great character. Often rescued from other old farmhouses, here they continue in another guise, recapturing the romance of country living as it once was.

LEFT & RIGHT *Despite the replacement of the old thatched roof with a replica one in tin, the house retains great character. Residents Douglas and Kiyo Woodruff have spent twenty years restoring the once-neglected house, a task that included the replastering of the exterior walls, which consist of a core of woven bamboo, built up with clay on either side. The* mon, *or gate, leading to the garden indicates that the farming family who once lived here were quite prosperous.*

OPPOSITE *The* engawa, *or veranda, which provides an intermediate space between the interior and the garden – once wrapped around the entire house but now only one section remains. Farmhouses like this were designed for summer living, and the sliding doors of the* engawa *encouraged maximum airflow.*

ABOVE *As evening falls, the Woodruffs set out candles and candlelit lanterns to recreate the ambience of old Japan. The couple added a timber deck, which extends from their bedroom at the rear of the house and provides a tranquil place for enjoying an early-evening cup of tea.*

RIGHT *One of the tatami rooms, which converts from sitting room during the day to bedroom in the evening. Here a few of the Woodruffs' eclectic antiques are diplayed, including a Tasiho-era (1912–1926) undergarment, worn under a kimono. It is patterned with horses and racing tickets, and is indicative of the modern Western craze sweeping Japan at the time. In the corner is an antique urn from Shigaraki.*

RIGHT *The farmhouse is filled with authentic details, which add to its character – from the earth-floored entrance with its aged wooden doors, to an old woven basket bearing a sprig from the garden, to the wood-fired stove in the kitchen, beside which sits a tiny figurine representing one of the seven Japanese gods of happiness.*

OPPOSITE *A rare sight in Japan is this circular bath, heated by an external wood-fuelled stove. In winter, yuzu (a type of native lime) from the garden adds a fragrant touch.*

LEFT & BELOW *An impressive lacquered elm* mizuya dansu, *or kitchen dresser, dominates one wall of a tatami guest room. This was once the tea room into which nobles were welcomed through a special entrance. The* dansu *holds a diverse collection of porcelain, including antique blue and white Imari ware and bolder contemporary pieces by local potter Kami Miki.*

旅
館

◖◗ the traditional inn

In pockets of ancient Kyoto, the architectural fabric of the old Imperial capital can still be glimpsed. Wedged between Shijo dori and the rambling Nishiki food market lies one such example – a neighbourhood of Meiji-era townhouses, or *machiya*. Each house is slightly different in character, yet with their uniform use of materials and proportions all blend into coherent and harmonious blocks. If not for the distinctive lamp bearing the characters for 'Kinmata', a passer-by could easily miss one of Kyoto's most enduring traditional inns, or *ryokans*.

In keeping with its origins as a family house, Kinmata has retained its original layout and character, its owner refusing to make too many concessions to contemporary life, or to the demands of running an inn. Haruji Ukai is the seventh generation of his family to live in the house, and for this reason prizes Kinmata as his ancestral home above all else. Yet it is this same stubborn refusal to change that imbues the *ryokan* with such authenticity. Much like the surrounding houses, Kinmata is a two-storey structure built from cypress and pine. Set almost flush with the narrow pavement, it presents an impenetrable face to the street with its slatted wooden façade and discreet entrance door. Inside, however, everything is designed to create a sense of quiet, harmony and escape from the busy city outside. This, after all, is the role of the *ryokan*, and one that Kinmata perfectly fulfils.

The process of allowing visitors to unwind completely begins at the *genkan*, or foyer. Once through the sliding front door, guests enter a broad space paved with flagstones and kept beautifully simple, but for a seasonal flower arrangement and a neat row of shoes, discarded by the wearer before stepping up into the

旅
館

interior of the house and into a pair of waiting slippers. This transitional space between outside and inside also provides the backdrop for the all-important social interaction between guests and host. It is here that guests are first greeted, and here, too, that they are bade farewell. The *genkan* of any *ryokan* is a vital aesthetic arena, setting the scene for what is to come. In the case of Kinmata, the interior of the inn appears simple in conception, but reveals refinement in tiny details – the quality of the aged wood or the delicate pattern of a *fusuma* door. On the ground floor, the house unfolds as a series of rooms arranged off a single central corridor, its wooden flooring worn smooth from the soft pad of slippered feet over two centuries.

The corridor slips discreetly past kitchen and dining room to skirt a tiny inner garden, essentially an open-air courtyard that allows daylight into the otherwise darkened interior. The garden also acts as both a physical and psychological pause for guests before the corridor leads them further into the house – to one of the guest rooms on the ground floor, which open out on to a rear outdoor garden; or upstairs to further guest rooms, which overlook the garden. Here in the guest quarters the experience of the *ryokan* is most intensely felt. Rooms are perfectly simple, with tatami floors, a low table surrounded by floor-level seating and a cupboard, fronted by sliding *fusuma* doors, which conceals a stack of thick futons, to be laid out as evening falls. It is left to the tiny details to impress: the flowers arranged in the alcove, the glimmer of lanterns in the garden beyond, or the care with which the cotton kimono has been folded and arranged beside the mirrored dressing stand

LEFT & FAR LEFT *Kinmata's slatted wooden façade and overhanging tiled eaves are typical of the* machiya, *or townhouses, in this part of old Kyoto. Only the lamp bearing the characters for 'Kinmata' mark it as a* ryokan, *or inn. The paved area outside is washed clean each morning with water from a bamboo bucket.*

OPPOSITE & BELOW RIGHT *A long corridor runs from the entrance to the very end of the building. It is broken halfway along its course by a miniature courtyard garden – called a* tsubo *– which allows daylight to enter the ground floor and provides a leafy outlook for the second-storey rooms.*

BELOW LEFT *A larger garden at the rear of the inn shows off the last fleeting hints of autumn colour. Although compact, it contains all the typical aesthetic requirements of the Japanese garden: a gravel yard, path with stepping stones, a stone lantern, ornamental rocks and a bamboo fence.*

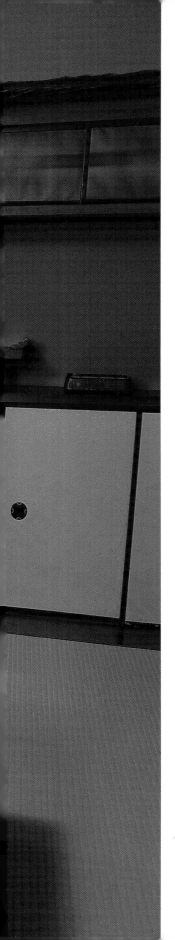

LEFT **&** BELOW *One of only eleven guest rooms at Kinmata, this one enjoys a full view of the garden. The room is designed to offer the experience of staying as an honoured guest in someone's home, from the antique scroll and fresh flowers placed in the* tokonoma *alcove to the table set with fine teacups.*

OPPOSITE *A view from the rear garden enables a full appreciation of the structure. The raised floor, referred to as* yuka, *stems back to the architectural style that evolved in Japan in the Yayoi period (300 BC – AD 300) to deal with monsoon conditions. Before the Meiji Restoration of 1868, second storeys were only permitted for aristocratic houses or inns.*

ABOVE *Architectural elegance is revealed in the exterior details at Kinmata. The design of the* engawa, *or veranda, railings allows the sunlight to create pleasing shadows throughout the day. The timber facing of an upstairs* demado, *or bay window, gives yet another opportunity for the aesthetic interplay of horizontal and vertical lines.*

LEFT & ABOVE *As evening falls, staff at the* ryokan *pull futons and bedding from cupboards concealed behind sliding* fusuma *doors. A guest returns from a day out to find the low table and seats removed to one side and a futon laid out in their place. A thick* kaki-buton, *or quilt, on top of the futon provides warmth. An antique lacquered* andon, *or floor lamp, is set alongside; as is a carefully folded cotton kimono, called a* yukata, *and waist tie.*

 RIGHT & OPPOSITE

*Although located in the
bustling centre of Kyoto,
Kinmata has an air of peace
and tranquillity, due in large
part to the clever use of
intermediate indoor-outdoor
spaces. At the upper level, a
narrow* engawa, *or veranda,
with railings helps to bring
nature indoors and provides
space for admiring the garden
courtyard below. The veranda
at ground level offers a
place for unwinding with a
game of mah jong.*

武家屋敷

 LEFT & ABOVE LEFT *Although a samurai house, it was built in the farmhouse style, with a hipped and gabled thatch roof. As his fortunes dwindled, the samurai living here changed profession to become a doctor. After curing one of Kyoto's most influential priests, the priest, in gratitude, arranged for the city limits to be extended to take in this remote area to the north of Kyoto – enabling the owner to enjoy the privileges of living within the city precincts. The gold-leafed ginkgo tree – which stands next to the original* kura, *or*

storehouse – was probably planted as a guardian to the house at the time of its construction in 1657. It is thought to have helped preserve the house over the centuries by acting as a lightning conductor.

ABOVE RIGHT *The commoners' entrance is immediately recognisable by its earthen floor, while the neighbouring entrance for aristocrats and samurai is accessed by wooden steps. The antique decorative screen, known as a* suitate, *is designed to screen prying eyes from the interior of the house.*

BELOW & RIGHT *While the informal garden at the front of the house (below) was restored to its original state, the courtyard garden (right) was redesigned by landscape gardener Marc Keane. Using traditional materials such as white gravel, cedar moss and raked sand, Keane created a meditative garden with the rhythmic motion of the waves as its theme.*

 RIGHT & BELOW *In keeping with the original plan of the house, the front room is reserved for tea ceremony. Here it is set with a brazier and antique silk screen. The lamp-lit shoin window, intended as a kind of writing desk, is a typical feature of a samurai home. A built-in hearth (below) also serves as a site where tea masters John McGee and Alexandre Avdulov conduct tea ceremony. The sixteenth-century iron kettle is one of their many beautiful tea utensils.*

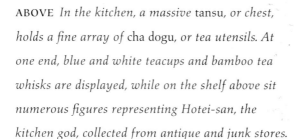

ABOVE *In the kitchen, a massive* tansu, *or chest, holds a fine array of* cha dogu, *or tea utensils. At one end, blue and white teacups and bamboo tea whisks are displayed, while on the shelf above sit numerous figures representing Hotei-san, the kitchen god, collected from antique and junk stores.*

OPPOSITE *As was typical of kitchens in substantial Japanese houses built prior to the twentieth century, the massive stove was wood-fired and comprised a series of built-in cooking pots, each a different size and fitted with a wooden lid. Around the stove, parts of the original earthenware floor are still visible.*

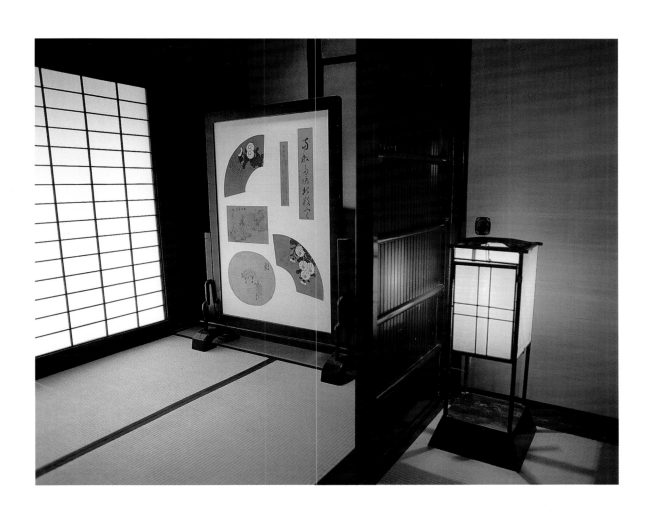

 LEFT & ABOVE *From its derelict state in the 1970s the house has been completely restored, with new floors laid and the walls replastered. It now offers a unique look at living style in the mid-seventeenth century, albeit with a few concessions to modern-day comfort, such as electricity and plumbing. In most other ways it remains true to the original design and ambience.*

民家

⊜ t h a t c h e d   m i n k a

Neither the lexicons of architecture nor history can adequately describe the 200-year-old farmhouse of Hiroyuki and Chikako Shindo. Despite its obvious architectural value – as one of a dwindling number of original thatched buildings still in situ in Japan's mountain villages – it is the role of the house as studio and creative space that is most intriguing. As the archetypal residence of traditional folk life, the thatched *minka*, or people's house, is a fitting spiritual home for the exponent of a classic folk art.

Hiroyuki Shindo is an acknowledged master of *aizen*, or indigo dyeing. He is one of a handful of artist-craftsmen who still produce indigo fabrics in the ancient manner, and his house plays a crucial part in the process. Symbolically, perhaps, the entrance to the farmhouse also marks the starting point for the time-consuming indigo-dyeing process. Here, in a barn-like space where farm animals once sheltered through the deep mountain winters, is a dyeing studio filled with sixteen *aigame,* traditional ceramic indigo vats set into the earthen floor. Every winter Shindo takes delivery of bundles of fermented indigo leaves – grown by one of the few remaining indigo farmers in Japan – and transfers them to the *aigame* for a second fermentaion. To help the process along, he adds a mixture of lime, bran, sake and ash. The ash is a crucial ingredient and is one of the hardest to find, but the house provides a ready supply.

Both the studio and the open-plan living space that opens from it are heated solely by wood-burning stoves. Between them they produce more than enough ash for the indigo fermentation. (The stoves, with their

chimneys rising up into the roof space, also serve to fumigate the thatch.) When the fermentation is complete, the indigo liquid is drained and used to dye specially woven linen, cotton and silk with Shindo's trademark delicacy of graded colour and tone. The design and dyeing process both take place in the studio.

Evidence of the artist's works are displayed in the adjoining living area, entered through a wall of sliding wooden screens. This interior space combines a kitchen, lounge/dining area and attic bedroom, with one entire wall of sliding glass doors offering views of the garden and mountain vistas beyond. Each of the tatami mats lining the floor is edged with distinctive indigo blue fabric, while an exquisitely dyed wall-hanging dominates the alcove in place of the typical scroll or flower arrangement. Shindo's work likewise finds its way into domestic use, whether in the form of *noren* curtains in a doorway or a thick quilted cloth covering the low table where eating and entertaining take place. There is little else here to distract the eye or mind, save for the original blackened wall and ceiling timbers of the farmhouse.

Even the indigo waste product has a use in this organic environment. The indigo sludge is used as compost for the garden; the water, for irrigation of the vegetable patch; and the ash, reused as a glaze for the beautiful grey-blue ceramics made by Chikako Shindo. Both Chikako and Hiroyuki relish the opportunity to explore the Japanese tradition of living as one with nature – not only in their day-to-day existence in the thatched farmhouse but, more especially, through their respective arts.

RIGHT *Heavy snow silhouettes the distinctive lines of the traditional thatched minka. Like its neighbours in this tiny, remote mountain village, it is thatched from grass that grows in the same valley. The ornamented ridge that runs the length of the roof is typical of* minka *architecture. The roof is so steep, with such deep eaves, that walls are barely visible.*

OPPOSITE & BELOW *The thick thatch of the* minka *is bound to a framework of* susudake *bamboo, which has turned black after years of smoke rising from the open hearth at floor level below. (Open hearths in these old country houses have now been largely replaced by stoves with chimneys.) The gable end of the roof ridge is adorned with the Shindo family crest, and incorporates a vent for expelling smoke from the hearth.*

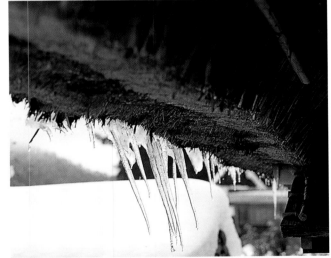

RIGHT **&** FAR RIGHT *The smoke-blackened timbers and the stark white walls and* shoji *screens of the old house create a dramatic backdrop for Hiroyuki Shindo's acclaimed indigo art. The wall-hanging in the* tokonoma *is typical of his style, as are the mat below and the decorative spheres. To the left of the alcove, a* shoin *window with carved transom – once the preserve of the samurai class – hints at the history of the house, built for a village chief who also collected taxes for the local warlord.*

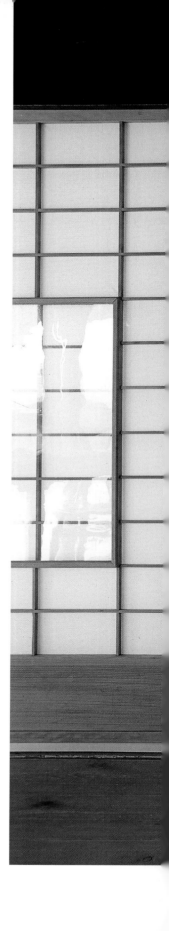

 LEFT & BELOW *Graduated, indigo-dyed linen screens hang at the entrance to the veranda, gently screening the strong afternoon sun that floods the house and helping to protect the tatami floor mats. At the same time, this diaphanous fabric wall allows views of the garden and village beyond, including the neighbouring* minkas, *with their snow-covered thatched roofs.*

RIGHT & OPPOSITE *Like the subtle gradations of tone found in Hiroyuki Shindo's indigo-dyed fabrics, the wood surfaces in the house reveal an equally varied patina. Red-toned cedar doors in the living room slide back to reveal a stepped chest of drawers, called a* kaidan dansu *(which leads to a sleeping loft); the cedar walls of the dining area are coloured ebony from two centuries of smoke from the cooking hearth (now replaced by a wood-burning stove); and a gold-toned cypress* mizuya dansu, *or kitchen dresser, provides ample household storage space.*

岐阜の農家

⊜ farmhouse reconstruction

The coastal town of Kamakura is famed for one of Japan's most impressive ancient engineering feats – the Daibutsu, or Giant Buddha. Much less known is the home of antique dealer and architect Yoshihiro Takishita. For other reasons entirely, it too is considered something of a masterpiece in construction terms. Approached through the narrow winding lanes of the old town, lined with early nineteenth-century villas, Takishita's house is set high on a hill overlooking the bay. It comprises two buildings that serve both as home to his immediate and extended family, as well as show space for his antiques business.

What is most unusual is that each of the buildings is an eighteenth-century farmhouse from Japan's snow country, the mountainous interior of Fukui prefecture. Each has been taken apart and transferred, literally, piece by piece to its new home in Kamakura. Instead of reassembling them exactly as they stood in their native terrain, Takishita has rebuilt them according to his needs, incorporating modern comforts without compromising the integrity of the original structures.

The oldest of the two restored farnmhouses dates from 1734. Its massive, open ground-floor level provides a dramatic gallery for the rare antique screens that Takishita sells to collectors around the world. Where once a farmer's family would have slept and eaten communally, now exquisite, hand-painted folding screens are displayed. Upstairs, where 250 years ago hay and food would have been stored, a series of rooms built into the steeply pitched roof offer guest accommodation and a study.

Across the leafy garden stands the second of the farmhouses, dating from the late 1700s. This is the family house, and in design is much like its older neighbour. The ground floor is largely taken up with an expansive open living area, with adjoining modern kitchen, bathroom and bedroom. The loft has been given over to storage of Takishita's cache of antique screens. A contemporary yet discreet extension provides additional bedrooms and family living space.

Both farmhouse buildings are notable for their exposed post-and-beam structure – testament to the skill and intuitive knowledge of Japan's mountain carpenters. A single massive central beam runs the full length of each house, intersected with tenon and mortis joints by a series of vertical posts. Adding strength to the central beam is its natural curvature. This key structural timber – typically elm or pine – would have been carefully selected from mountain forests in the middle of winter, felled and slid down the snowy slopes. In the valley it would have been left to dry out for two to three years, until the carpenter finally deemed it ready to use and construction began. Irregularities in the tree's huge, naturally curved trunk were exploited by the carpenters to add strength and beauty to the interior structure.

Nearly all of the timber in both houses is original, the pine floors and ceiling timbers stained black from years of smoke and ash from the farmer's hearth. It is the juxtaposition of such essentially rustic elements with Takishita's wonderfully refined furnishings and artwork that gives his home such aesthetic impact.

⊜ **ABOVE & RIGHT** *Secluded in a leafy garden, high above the historic town of Kamakura, sits the unusual home of Yoshihiro Takishita, who transported two farmhouses from the mountainous interior of Japan and reconstructed them here. The earliest of the two houses, which dates from 1734, is entered through a traditional* mon, *or gate. Across the garden is the second house, which dates from the late 1700s. Although the original thatched roofs have been replaced, the steep pitch of the roofline remains. The houses were rescued by Takishita just days before the village where they stood was to be flooded for a dam project.*

OPPOSITE *In the oldest of the two farmhouses, the vast area under the roof has been converted into two levels of living space. This small sitting room is nestled under soot-blackened wooden beams bound with rice-straw rope. The steep pitch of the roof is typical of houses from Japan's snow country.*

BELOW *One corner of the upper level has been converted into a secluded study, with shelving and cupboards discreetly built in, and heating installed under the floorboards. This is typical of the way architect Yoshihiro Takishita has reworked the old farmhouses to make a comfortable home.*

BELOW & RIGHT *A tatami room in the late eighteenth-century farmhouse serves as a guest room. Low folding screens were traditionally arranged next to the futon to shield the guest from draughts. This particular screen depicts a hedge of chrysanthemums and dates fom the eighteenth century. It is one of many screens bought and sold by Yoshihiro Takishita in his antiques business.*

LEFT & BELOW *A distinctive feature of both farmhouses is the huge, rough-hewn ceiling beams that span the entire width of each structure. The pine wood throughout the houses has been blackened by centuries of wood smoke from the open hearths, which were common in country homes. It now acts as a dramatic backdrop for Yoshihiro Takishita's furniture and art, whether a nineteenth-century Chinese dining table lacquered with gold leaf (opposite) or any of the exquisite pieces dsiplayed in Takishita's antiques showroom (below left and right).*

吉田山荘

◈ imperial villa

The Imperial villa is one of the classic forms of Japanese architecture, and one of the oldest. Its origins go back to the very beginnings of building in Japan – to the shrine that housed the spirits of shamanistic gods, from which the emperors are said to have descended. Over the centuries, of course, the Imperial villa has evolved along with each new architectural style. One of the most extraordinary and little-known examples is a 1930s villa inspired by the Art Deco movement – Yoshida Sanso.

This expansive two-storey villa, built entirely from Japanese cypress and tile, is surrounded by landscaped gardens and sited on a hill with views of Kyoto's mountains. It was constructed in the early 1930s for Emperor Hirohito's brother-in-law, Prince Higashi Fushiminomiya, as a convenient base for attending his studies at nearby Kyoto University. Japan in the 1920s and early 1930s was a time of great change – of embracing the new and the modern. Few styles symbolised that modernity as boldly as Art Deco. After making its debut in 1925 at the Exposition Internationale des Arts Décoratifs et Industriels Modernes in Paris, Art Deco spread rapidly across Europe, America and Asia, where it made its impact felt in Japan especially, inspiring the art world and popular culture alike. This makes perfect sense, given the parallels between Art Deco and traditional Japanese aesthetics – in particular, the strong sense of spatial unity and awareness and the impulse to incorporate art into daily life, especially home life. It was only natural, then, that an Imperial family member should be seen to be at the forefront of this exciting new artistic development.

吉田山荘

Yet, despite its modern source of inspiration, Yoshida Sanso is deeply rooted in ancient Imperial tradition. Even the street entrance to the long driveway is marked by a towering *tori* gate, which is usually found on shrine premises to indicate a holy site. The wood used for the construction of the villa itself is *kiso hinoki* – a type of cypress grown in a particular valley in Nagano for the rebuilding of Ise Shrine, the most venerable of shrine monuments, which is destroyed and built anew every thirty years in an age-old Shinto purification ritual. The cypress trees cultivated in these Nagano forest plots are raised expressly for this purpose, but were also used in this instance for the building of the new Imperial villa.

No expense was spared for the construction. Floors were laid in the finest cuts of oak and cherry, and the most talented artists and craftspeople of the day were employed to install the interior detailing. Stained-glass windows were designed to incorporate the initials of the young Imperial bachelor, floor tiles were specially made bearing the Imperial crest of the chrysanthemum, as were door pulls and wall lights. Furnishings, too, were commissioned – some for the Japanese-style tatami-mat rooms, other pieces for the Western-style rooms.

Fortunately, little has changed since Yoshida Sanso was built for its Imperial resident. All of the original Art Deco features have been preserved and restored by its present owners, Hideichi and Kyoko Nakamura, who have nurtured the villa back to life. Kyoko in particular has taken a keen interest in maintaining the exquisite interior features, and the spirit of artistic endeavour that first inspired the villa.

🌼 ABOVE **&** RIGHT *The approach to the villa is through an enormous* tori *gate, a structure that typically marks the entrance to a shrine precinct. From here, a steep driveway sweeps up to the two-storey villa, which was constructed from cypress according to ancient tenets – not a single nail was used. Despite its substantial size, the villa gives an impression of lightness, created by the gentle upswing of the eaves. Each roof tile bears the Imperial symbol of the sixteen-petalled chrysanthemum.*

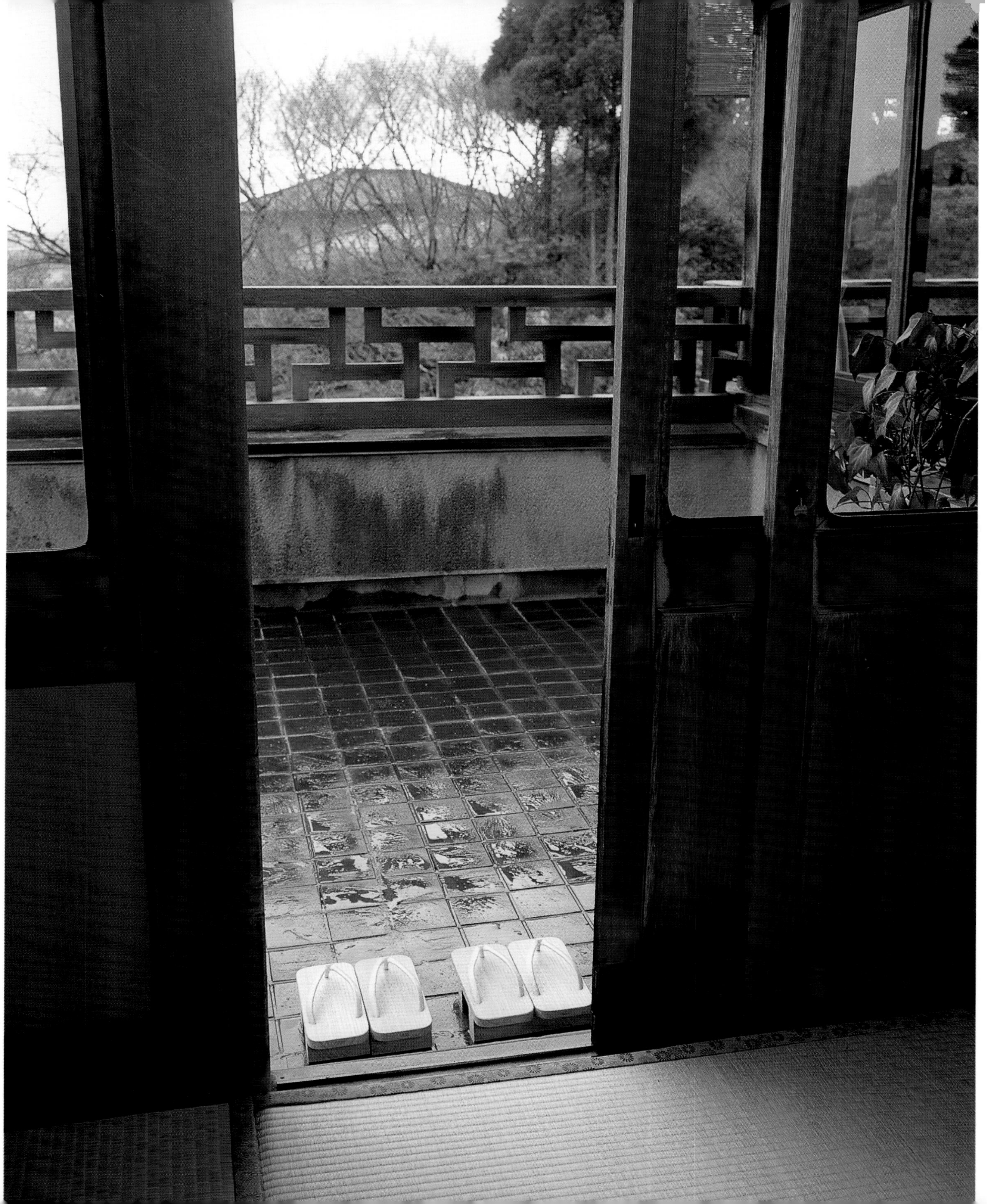

 *OPPOSITE* *The villa is run by its owners as a discreet* ryokan. *Rooms on the upper level open on to a veranda overlooking the garden and with views to the Kyoto hills. The design of the veranda railing is an amalgam of Art Deco and Japanese elements.*

ABOVE *Wooden* geta *sit ready in the* genkan, *or foyer, for those venturing out to the garden. The* genkan *is paved with earthenware tiles, some bearing the Imperial symbol of the chrysanthemum, commissioned especially for the villa.*

LEFT *What appears to be a simple tatami room is in fact designed to project an air of refinement befitting an Imperial villa. The tatami mats are edged with an elegant brocade, while the* tokonoma *alcove is in the formal* shoin *style of the nobility, with an unusual circular* shoji *window.*

ABOVE *In summer, the usual papered or glass* shoji *doors that separate the rooms from the veranda are replaced with ones made from woven reed. Designed to improve ventilation during the oppressive heat of the Kyoto summer, they also filter the sun to create the most delicate plays of light and shadow.*

BELOW & RIGHT *The main entrance to the* genkan *is marked by a pair of beautifully panelled* shoji *sliding doors. Their patterning is derived directly from Art Deco motifs, and illustrates the common sensibility shared by the modern art movement of the 1920s and 1930s and traditional Japanese aesthetics. Sliding* shoji *in the classic style divide the terracotta-paved* genkan *from the interior with its luxurious parquetry floor of oak and cherry.*

BELOW *This quintessential scene demonstrates the mutability of indoor and outdoor space. The sliding* shoji *walls of the interior room open on to the* engawa, *an intermediate space with glass doors opening on to the veranda and garden beyond.*

OPPOSITE *The villa is L-shaped in layout, with a small single-storey wing adjoining the main two-storey structure. The low railing edging the veranda is a particularly elegant touch and is derived from the ancient architecture of the Shinto shrine.*

 LEFT & BELOW *The attention paid to decorative detail by owner Kyoko Nakamura is clear in this elegant guest room, once used by Prince Fushimi. Reflecting its rarefied connections, the Imperial symbol of the chrysanthemum is evident in the carved transom, and in the* hikitei, *or handles, of the sliding* fusuma *doors. Nakamura continues the interior blend of Western and Japanese design with her table settings and handmade lamps.*

RIGHT *Stained-glass windows in the Art Deco style were commissioned especially. The motif in the long rectangular window, which is repeated around the perimeter of the circular window, is abstracted from the Japanese characters for 'Fushiminomiya', the prince for whom the villa was built.*

FAR RIGHT *More traditional decorative details echo the geometry of the Art Deco elements: a panelled ceiling, carved transom, and the play of vertical and horizontal lines evident in the shoji paper screen and outer wooden door.*

箱根の別荘

Among foreign admirers of Japanese architecture, the American Frank Lloyd Wright stands out as one of its most vigorous proponents. It is perhaps appropriate, then, that contemporary Japanese architects have in turn been inspired by Wright's take on their own native building style. Tokyo-based Eizo Shiina is one such architect. His work is universally underpinned by the ancient spirit of Japanese building, which has its origins in shrine and temple architecture, but with one project in particular he was also inspired by the monumental and organic work of Frank Lloyd Wright.

For the mountain retreat of fashion designer Yukiko Hanai, Shiina created a house, which, unusually for a Japanese home, has a solid and permanent presence, its heavy façade seemingly hewn from the mountain itself. At first glance the house seems to be quite at odds with the flexible style of the traditional Japanese building, with its typically light foundations and timber construction. It looks as though it might be more at home in the suburbs of Chicago – where Wright's houses made such an impression – than in the forests of Hakone, an area known for its hot-spring resorts and within view of venerable Mount Fuji.

Yet closer inspection reveals a strong debt to the essence of Japanese architecture. Like the Japanese builder, Wright sought to develop a unique brand of organic architecture in which both form and materials were at one with the site. Shiina has drawn on this legacy in his design for the Hakone house. Where traditional residential building would use lightweight timber, Shiina uses textured brick, inspired by Wright's pioneering

箱根の別荘

use of textured concrete. Like Wright, Shiina purposefully emphasises the texture of the building materials, and the relationship of the building to the environment is all-important.

Inside, Shiina draws on Wright's concepts of interior flow, the open floor plan and the dissolving of the boundaries between inside and outside elements that are also firmly rooted in the lexicon of Japanese architecture. Updating the Japanese device of sliding wooden screens, which can be pulled back to merge indoor and outdoor spaces, Shiina installed walls of glass in the main living area, providing a constant view of the forest outside and allowing the changing light conditions outside to register inside. These transparent movable walls slide back on metal tracks to give access to a long veranda, where humid summer days can be spent in the path of cool mountain breezes.

Alongside the Wright influence, Shiina is also inspired by the spatial philosophies of ancient Japan. The internal structure itself is directly taken from the pillar-and-beam construction of the Shinto shrine. Built from Canadian cedar, the massive interlinking timbers are exposed under the lofty roof height and the scent of the cedar permeates the house. Under this canopy, the living spaces flow rhythmically from one level to the next. In creating this mountain retreat, the architect has admirably filled his client's brief for a country house with a sense of rustic simplicity; a place that serves as a spiritual sanctuary. To his credit, he has brought these qualities to life in a building of great modernity and integrity, rooted in the ideas of ancient Japan.

OPPOSITE *A balcony wraps around the living area. In fine weather, massive glass doors can be slid smoothly back on concealed tracks to rest, invisibly, in a deep recess in the supporting pillar. This feature plays on the traditional sliding* shoji *door.*

ABOVE *Both the owner, Yukiko Hanai, and architect Eizo Shiina, wanted the house to be in harmony with its environment, to bring the outside and inside together. This enables the residents to feel as though they are nestled among the forests of Hakone.*

RIGHT *Although the ceiling above the main living room is vast, underfloor heating means that the room stays warm, even in the depths of winter.*

FAR RIGHT *The centrepiece of the living room is a dining table made especially for the house from Japanese oak. The centre panel pulls out to reveal a stove with three built-in gas rings, on which food can be cooked directly at the table. An overhead extractor chimney draws smoke and cooking odours up out of the room.*

 ABOVE *The architect's intention was that the layout of the house should have a fluid rhythm, revealing itself gradually. Thus the entrance opens to a mezzanine level, which leads upstairs to the living area and downstairs to the bedrooms and bathroom.*

LEFT *The house reveals its debt to ancient Japanese building principles in the internal structure of pillars and beams, which echoes that of temple and shrine architecture. All the internal timber is Canadian cedar.*

LEFT *An intimate tea-ceremony room with tatami floors leads off from the open-plan living area. Even in this quiet, more traditional space, Eizo Shiina's bold vertical windows help to unify the tea room with the rest of the house. As a fashion designer, owner Yukiko Hanai pays great attention to the aesthetic details of the house, changing the scroll and flower arrangement in the* tokonoma *as mood and season dictates.*

RIGHT *Yukiko Hanai's restrained taste is evident in her choice of scroll, depicting Daruma, the ancient Buddhist scholar, and a thousand-year-old vase holding sprigs of white camellia and plum blossom.*

BELOW *The bath and surrounding floor are made entirely from granite. Water is pumped directly from an underground thermal source nearby, to create a luxurious private* onsen, *or hot spring. Hakone is famed for its many hot-spring resorts, yet this site is shielded from any such intrusion.*

OPPOSITE *With glass walls that make the bathroom seem surrounded by trees, this room is a superb example of how the house has been designed to bring inside and outside together. The bathroom is understandably the owner's favourite place to unwind and relax after working all week in Tokyo.*

 LEFT *A collection of antique, vermilion-red lacquerware, which dates from between the fourteenth and sixteenthth centuries. The square plate was made around 1900 in the Oribe style by the celebrated potter Rozanjin Kitaoji.*

BELOW *This setting, called* yotsu-wan, *was traditionally used for food served to priests. The lids of both bowls are designed to be removed and upturned for use as plates.*

ABOVE *Yukiko Hanai wanted a simple house built from natural materials to serve as her weekend retreat and a spiritual sanctuary. A wooden post bears the name of the house, Kamui — from the Japanese characters for 'flower', 'mist' and 'living'.*

RIGHT *In the style of a Frank Lloyd Wright house, Kamui was built from textured brick, to harmonise with the natural environment. An early nineteenth-century stone statue from Korea stands at the approach to the front of the house.*

東京の家

In the crowded urban sprawl that is Japan's biggest city, it is a rare luxury indeed to boast more than the minimal amount of living space. `The typical family home might consist of little more than a modest lounge room, with small bedrooms and a tiny bathroom and kitchen. Yet one couple are fortunate enough to own space that is otherwise virtually unheard of in Tokyo. Yuko Saito and her husband enjoy the proportions of a vast country farmhouse. Dating from the eighteenth century, the house was transported from a mountain village, and then reassembled using much of the original timber along with new materials, which were sympathetically worked in with the old.

The house is the brainchild of Yoshihiro Takishita, who has built a reputation for his sensitive reconstruction of vintage farmhouses otherwise slated for demolition. With his help, Yuko Saito has created an environment that combines the character and patina of rustic Japan with a sophisticated modern sensibility that makes the house eminently comfortable and suited to life in Tokyo. Unifying the house throughout is the owner's passion for Japanese aesthetics.

As you would expect to find in a 200-year-old farmhouse, the ground floor is a large, open space dominated overhead by a solid ceiling beam that runs the full length of the room. The walls are of clay, newly rendered but using old techniques. Floor timbers are also new and conceal an underfloor heating system that extends throughout the house. This eliminates the need for unsightly modern radiator vents or freestanding

東京の家

heaters, thereby helping to maintain the character of old Japan. Unlike a rustic residence, however, is the sophisticated interior scheme installed by Saito. In part it seeks to recreate the refined atmosphere of Edo-era Japan (1603–1867), and in part it is intended to be modern in its streamlined functionality.

In the main living area, for example, a sleek suite of French leather sofas provide relaxed, low-level seating – while the adjoining dining area contains a table fashioned from an old storehouse door surrounded by antique English dining chairs. Around the room, specially designed cedar cabinetry conceals television and hi-fi system – a beautiful example of the modern carpenter's craft.

Against this discreet backdrop – a warm melding of zelkoba, pine and cypress woods – Yuko Saito displays her love of Japanese antiques. Some are special objects; other pieces were cheap finds picked up at temple markets. More treasured finds are displayed in the adjoining tatami room – a space reserved for formal tea ceremonies, or for guests to overnight. Gentle lighting comes from Edo-style wall lamps; their rice-paper shades create a warm opaque light that is ideally suited to showing off the rich timber tones of the house.

Upstairs, the structure and character of the farmhouse once again make their presence felt. High-pitched ceilings are lined with bamboo and yellow clay. A broad staircase leads to two spacious bedrooms – decorated with a clever mix of Western and Japanese furnishings. Architectural details enhance the feeling of space, with high ceilings and exposed beams creating an atmosphere more akin to that of the countryside than urban Tokyo.

LEFT *From the front gate, a neat stone path leads past a small
front garden to the simplest of doorways. In keeping
with the exterior of the old farmhouse from which this house
was converted, the façade features whitewashed clay walls,
constructed according to an old technique. Where possible,
original materials were used; but the idea was to create a new
house adapted to modern living, so new was mixed in with old.*

 LEFT & FAR LEFT *Instead of planting an ornamental garden – the more usual style for an urban residence – Yuko Saito was inspired by the rural origins of the house and sourced all the garden plants from the mountains in Chiba prefecture. The overall effect, with the meandering gravel paths, bound bamboo fencing and informal plantings, is one of great charm and rustic simplicity. A* seki butsu, *or stone Buddha, in the garden is 400 years old and was inherited by Yuko Saito from her father.*

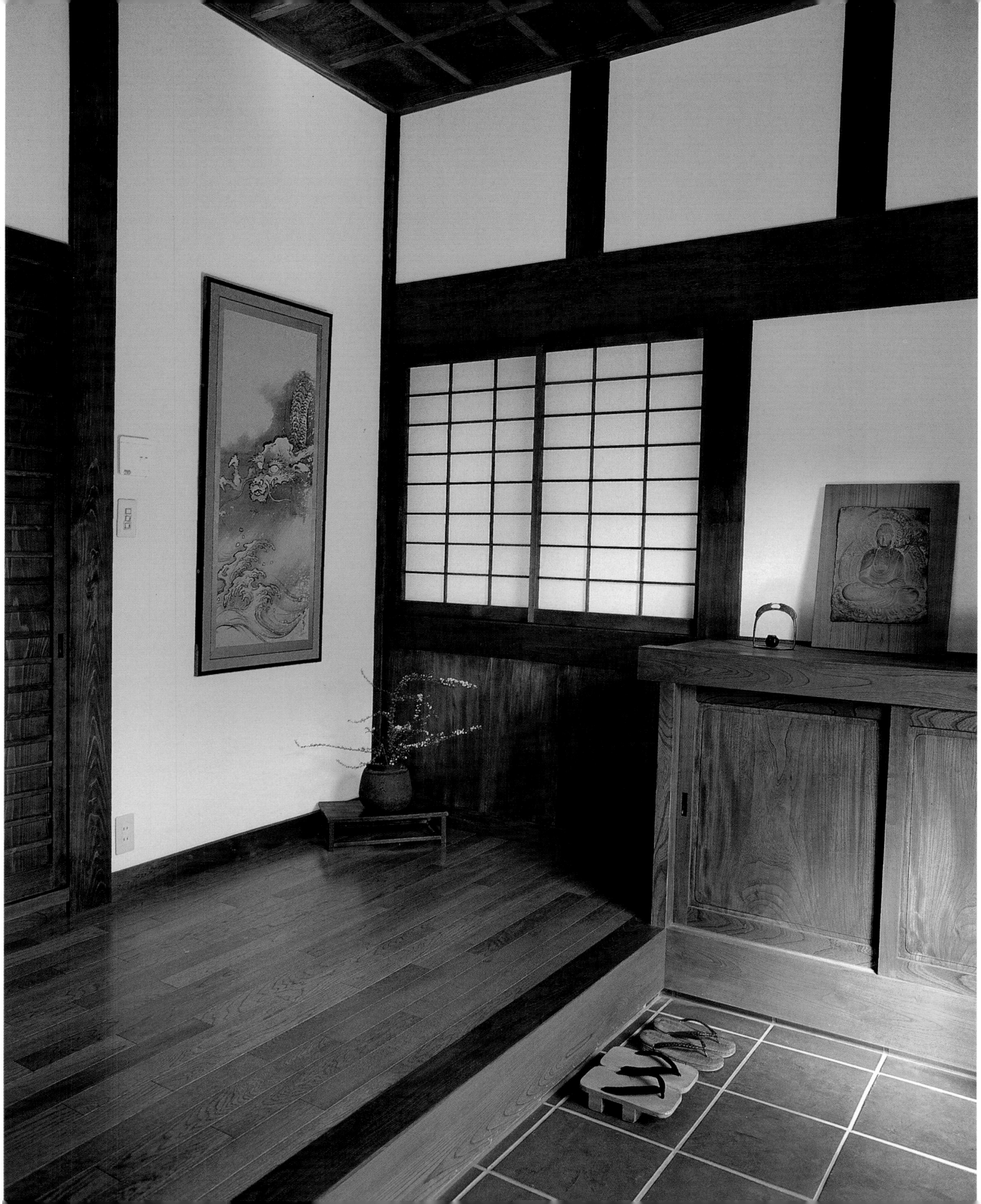

 OPPOSITE *As the place where visitors are welcomed to the house, the genkan, or foyer, provides an important social space. Yuko Saito uses the area to display pertinent pieces of art that relate to the time of year, or perhaps a particular festival. The flower arrangement is also changed regularly.*

ABOVE *In the genkan, a custom-built storage cupboard with sliding doors blends in seamlessly with the aged farmhouse timbers. Shoes and house slippers are kept inside, enabling a smooth transition from outside to inside. For stepping out into the garden, a wooden pair of geta sit ready.*

 ABOVE & OPPOSITE *Under a sloping country-style ceiling, a staircase of Nara pine leads upstairs from the ground level. In contrast with the pristine, whitewashed clay walls, the textural interest and gold tones of the ceiling add great charm and warmth. The ceiling is made from bamboo and yellow clay and was reconstructed from the original farmhouse building, using new materials along with some of the original aged bamboo.*

OPPOSITE & BELOW LEFT *Although furnished with a Western-style bed, the mood of Yuko Saito's bedroom is overwhelmingly Japanese. At the end of the bed sits a low table for calligraphy, set with inks and antique writing utensils, and a brush stand.*

BELOW RIGHT *An elegant interior window above the bed opens to the hallway to allow more light, as well as better ventilation, in the summer months. It features an old-fashioned* otoshi, *or drop lock, which secures the two sections of the window in place.*

LEFT & BELOW *Lounge and dining areas occupy a single vast space underneath the 200-year-old ceiling beams of the original farmhouse. French leather sofas and English dining chairs sit beautifully with Japanese pieces like the dining and coffee tables, made from old wooden doors. The hanging screen dates from the early-nineteenth century and is intended to create a sense of space, with its open view of treetops and flying sparrows.*

OPPOSITE & BELOW *The bathroom epitomises Yuko Saito's clever mix of ages-old Japanese aesthetics and modern practicality. Modelled on the traditional Japanese o-furo, yet with the advantage of modern plumbing, the bathroom resembles a miniature bathhouse, with a tiled, drained floor – where the bather perches on a wooden stool to soap up, wash and rinse – and a cypress tub for soaking. One wall is entirely of glass, offering views to the garden beyond, yet screened by reed blinds.*

現代の家

japanese modern

On the face of it, modern Japanese architecture often seems far removed from the architecture of ancient Japan, which was the primary influence on residential building over the centuries. In place of lightweight timber structures and sliding *shoji* screens are massive concrete façades and fixed spatial perimeters. Perhaps because the materials and basic elements of the Japanese house remained unchanged right up until the middle of last century, the new look pioneered by architects such as Arata Isozaki and Tadao Ando comes as a shock. Yet often the concepts underlying avant-garde houses are a direct continuation of architectural tradition.

One house in Gumma prefecture, east of Tokyo, designed by architect Eizo Shiina, embodies the culture of ancient Japan in a very contemporary way. Set amidst a swath of rice fields, the house is unobtrusive. It is contained within a low white wall, with only two tiny peaked roofs and a cluster of green treetops protruding above. The exterior is reminiscent of the eighteenth-century houses of samurai, who traditionally encircled their homes with whitewashed mud-brick walls – partly for security, but also to hide the fact that their houses were not nearly as grand as those of the aristocrats to whose level they aspired. Inside these particular white walls, however, nothing could be further from the truth.

The perimeter walls are not there to shield prying eyes or to hide an inferior house. Instead, they have been designed to serve as an integral part of the overall building. In this sense, the house is an organic whole: there are no separate, freestanding elements *per se*, and every space within those white walls is intrinsically

現代の家

linked. The boundaries between indoors and outdoors have been intentionally removed. The traditional devices of sliding *shoji* doors to the garden and the *engawa,* or veranda – both of which serve to expand the interior living space – have here been taken to their logical conclusion.

The house comprises two narrow wings joined by a large open courtyard that creates an 'outer room'. This is by far the largest spatial component, indicating its importance in the overall scheme of the house. The indoor spaces seem dwarfed by comparison. Each of the interior wings serves a different purpose – one is for communal access and is completely open-plan, with kitchen and living area worked into a unified whole. Across the courtyard, or 'outer room', is the 'private' wing, containing two bedrooms, a bathroom and a tea room. The only apparent way to cross between the two wings is to walk across the 'outer room', thereby enhancing the breakdown between indoor and outdoor space. In a departure from Japanese building convention, this idea has been applied not just horizontally, but vertically as well.

Extraordinarily, the house is largely open to the skies, or at least that is the illusion created by the architect's masterful reworking of vernacular materials. Apart from the 'outer room', over which there is no covering at all, the living area is covered by a ceiling of traditional woven reed, which filters the daylight above to throw dappled shadows around the walls and floor. The bathroom has a transparent ceiling, while only the tea room has a solid, opaque ceiling – ironically designed to mimic the pattern of a traditional sliding *shoji* door.

RIGHT *Although dynamic and highly modern in appearance, the white walls of this house recall a much earlier architectural tradition – that of the clay whitewashed walls that typically encircled a samurai home in the eighteenth century. These walls are made using a particular type of mortar mixed with ground marble.*

 OPPOSITE & ABOVE LEFT *The central courtyard is referred to by the architect as an 'outer room' because it is designed as an extension of the interior living space – an essential part of the home. Even during winter, this 'outer room' acts as a sun trap.*

ABOVE RIGHT *In the bathroom, the boundary between indoors and outdoors has all but been removed. With a transparent ceiling and glass wall that opens on to a private patio, the room is flooded with daylight, making garden and bathroom as one.*

LEFT *In fine weather, the reed blinds along the passageway can be raised to create an additional living area for sunbathing or lounging. Woven reed blinds also hang the full frontage of the internal living area, and can be adjusted to any length.*

BELOW *One wing of the house is occupied by an open living and dining area with cherry wood floors. The woven reed ceiling is protected by an outer layer of corrugated polycarbonate and translucent insulation sheeting, which allows daylight to enter.*

 OPPOSITE *With its flexible walls of woven reed, the side passageway can be converted into any number of guises, to control the light at any time of day. In this respect it resembles the traditional engawa, or veranda, with its sliding screens.*

ABOVE *Almost the full length of the interior living-room wall is inset with sliding glass doors, a modern reinterpretation of the shoji. These massive glass doors can be slid back noiselessly on their floor tracks, to be fully concealed within a deep cavity.*

BELOW *Woven reed has been used for centuries in Japanese homes. When fashioned into blinds and sliding doors, it is perfectly suited to Japan's humid summers, allowing air to circulate while screening out insects and the fiercest of the sun's rays.*

OPPOSITE *Another native plant that has been inventively applied to the Japanese house – bamboo. There are some 118 varieties of bamboo in Japan, once said to have had over 1400 uses. Here, split bamboo mats line the floor of the bathroom.*

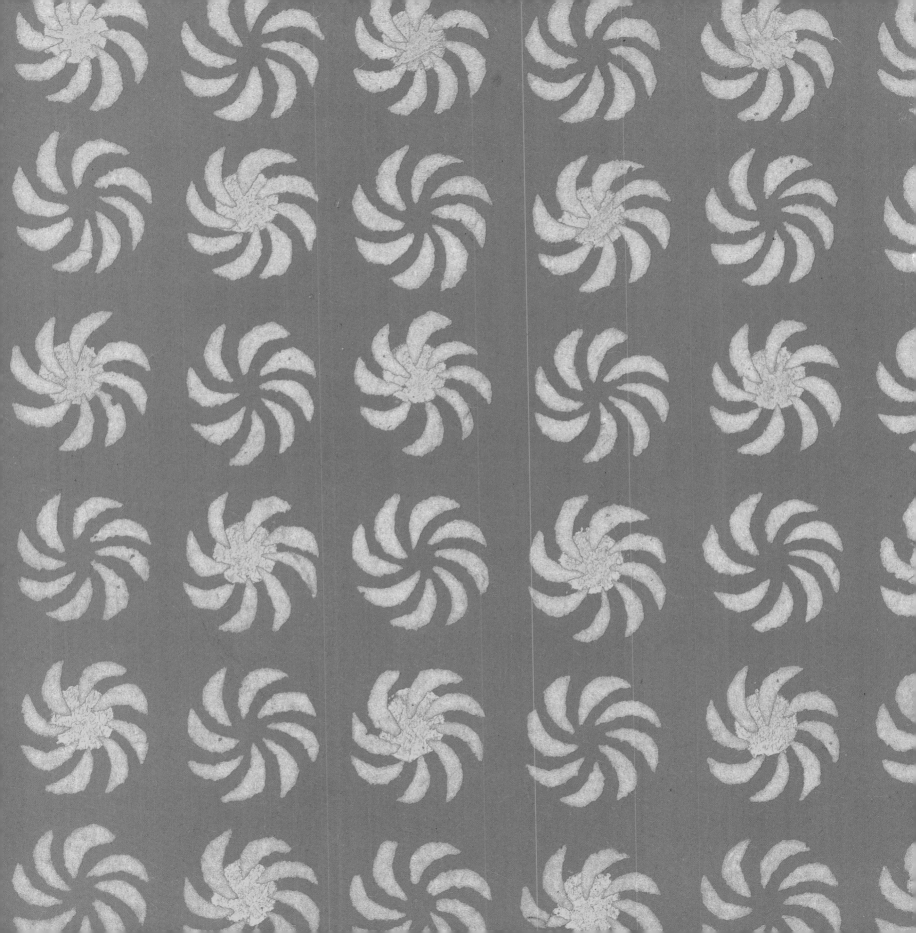

acknowledgments

The author and publisher would like to thank the following for their kind assistance :

Keiko Shima, Takako Omi, Professor Masami Kobayashi, Kinu Shigeyama, Naoki & Reiko Ando, Kimiko Yamada, Yoshihiro and Reiko Takishita, Nikki Twyman, Yukiko Hanai, Yoshiyuki Hanai, Eiko Ishikawa, David and Tomoko Guilfoile, Yuko Saito, Eizo Shiina, Koki Umezu, Fusae Kojima, John McGee, Alexander Avdulov, Nakahigashi Hisato, Douglas and Kiyo Woodruff, Kyoko Nakamura, Soren Bisgaard, Marc Keane, Nakamura Sotetsu, Sen Futessai Soshu, Hisanori Saeki and all at Mushakoji Senke, Hiroyuki and Chikako Shindo, Haruji Ukai, Itsuka Fukumura, Hajime Nishimura. Special thanks to Noboru Murata, Lina Wang, Deanne Gedge, Arisa Tanaka, Yoko Dohi, Mina Ohtsuka and Kyoko Matsuda.

The decorations accompanying each chapter are traditional Japanese architectural motifs symbolising the following:
page 14: pestles; *page 30:* coin with wave pattern; *page 44:* shrine gate; *page 62:* city; *page 76:* rice field; *page 90:* balance weight; *page 106:* plum; *page 120:* divining marks; *page 134:* two bars; *page 146:* chrysanthemum; *page 164:* temple gong; *page 182:* nail puller; *page 200:* fan.